This Notebook Belongs to:

Made in the USA
Monee, IL
12 January 2022

88785292R00063